WEATHER WATCH

Winter

by Cynthia Amoroso and Robert B. Noyed

Winter is here! Winter is one of the four **seasons**. It comes after fall and before spring.

Winter is the first season of the year.

Winter is not the same everywhere. In some places, winter can be very cold. In other places, winter is warmer.

Deserts are usually warm in the winter.

When winter is cold, it can bring snow. When it snows, the ground and the trees become covered in white.

This forest is covered in snow.

Big storms can bring lots of snow. Strong winds blow the snow. These storms are called **blizzards**.

It is hard to see through the snow during a blizzard.

The cold winter air **freezes** water. A **layer** of ice forms on the tops of ponds and lakes.

In the winter, a layer of ice forms on lakes.

Winter can be a hard time for animals. It is not easy to find food. Some animals, such as bears, sleep through much of the winter.

A bear gets ready to sleep for the winter.

Some animals grow **thick** fur in the winter. This fur helps them stay warm.

Rabbits grow more fur in the winter.

Many people enjoy being outdoors during winter. Skiing is a favorite winter sport. It is fun to ice skate, too.

Children take a break from skiing.

Children play in the snow.
They like to make snowmen.
They slide down hills on sleds.

These children are having fun sledding.

Winter is the coldest season.
Snow is falling all around.
Have fun out in the snow!

A girl makes a snow angel.

Glossary

blizzards (BLIZ-urdz): Blizzards are big snowstorms. Blizzards bring lots of snow.

freezes (FREEZ-ez): If something freezes, it turns from a liquid to a solid. Water freezes to form ice.

layer (LAY-ur): A layer is a coating on something. A layer of ice forms over lakes in the winter.

seasons (SEE-zinz): Seasons are the four parts of the year. The four seasons are winter, spring, summer, and fall.

thick (THIK): If something is thick, it has many parts close together. In the winter, animals grow thick fur.

To Find Out More

Books

Branley, Franklyn M. *Sunshine Makes the Seasons*. New York: HarperCollins, 2005.

Roca, Nuria. *Winter*. Hauppauge, NY: Barron's, 2004.

Rockwell, Anne. *Four Seasons Make a Year.* New York: Walker & Co., 2004.

Web Sites

Visit our Web site for links about winter: *childsworld.com/links*

Note to Parents, Teachers, and Librarians: We routinely verify our Web links to make sure they are safe and active sites. So encourage your readers to check them out!

Index

About the Authors

Cynthia Amoroso has worked as an elementary school teacher and a high school English teacher. Writing children's books is another way for her to share her passion for the written word.

Robert B. Noyed has worked as a newspaper reporter and in the communications department for a Minnesota school district. He enjoys the challenge and accomplishment of writing children's books.

On the cover: Many snowmen are made during the winter.

Published by The Child's World®
1980 Lookout Drive • Mankato, MN 56003-1705
800-599-READ • www.childsworld.com

ACKNOWLEDGMENTS
The Child's World®: Mary Berendes, Publishing Director
The Design Lab: Design and production
Red Line Editorial: Editorial direction

PHOTO CREDITS: iStockphoto, cover, 7, 9, 19, 21; Robert Kohlhuber/
iStockphoto, 3; Michael Chen/iStockphoto, 5; Rolf Weschke/
iStockphoto, 11; Suzann Julien/iStockphoto, 13; Ben Renard-Wiart/
iStockphoto, 15; Marzanna Syncerz/iStockphoto, 17

Printed in the United States of America in Mankato, Minnesota.
July, 2010
PA02066

LIBRARY OF CONGRESS CATALOGING-IN-PUBLICATION DATA
Amoroso, Cynthia.
  Winter / by Cynthia Amoroso and Robert B. Noyed.
    p. cm. — (Weather watch)
  Includes index.
  ISBN 978-1-60253-366-0 (library bound : alk. paper)
  1. Winter—Juvenile literature. I. Noyed, Robert B. II. Title. III. Series.
  QB637.8.A46 2010
  508.2—dc22   2009030220